Drawing
on the Go!
Animals

Barbara Soloff Levy

Dover Publications, Inc.
Mineola, New York

Bibliographical Note

Drawing on the Go! Animals, first published by
Dover Publications, Inc., in 2010, is a republication in a different
format of the work originally published as *How to Draw Animals* by
Dover Publications, Inc., in 2008.

International Standard Book Number

ISBN-13: 978-0-486-47944-6
ISBN-10: 0-486-47944-7

Manufactured in the United States by LSC Communications
47944706   2020
www.doverpublications.com

Note

Would you like to learn to draw your favorite animal? It's easy! Follow the simple steps in this little book and you'll discover how to draw a quacking duck, a friendly cat, and even an enormous whale! Begin with the picture of the chick on page 2. You'll be doing some erasing, so use a pencil. First, draw an oval for the body, with a small circle for the head. Next, add the beak, the tail, and the outline of the wing. Erase the parts of the body that have a broken line. Now add the eye, the wing feathers, and the legs and feet. You've just drawn a chirping chicken!

2   Chick

Practice Page

4   Duck

Practice Page

6   Rooster

Practice Page

8   Goose

Practice Page

10 Swan

Practice Page

12   Cat

Practice Page

14   Leopard

Practice Page

16   Dog

Practice Page

18   Fox

Practice Page

Practice Page

22 Lamb

Practice Page

24 Cow

Practice Page

26   Deer

Practice Page

28 Moose

Practice Page

30 Horse

Practice Page

32　Zebra

Practice Page

34 Giraffe

Practice Page

36   Camel

Practice Page

38   Mouse

Practice Page

40   Squirrel

Practice Page

42   Rabbit

Practice Page

44 Porcupine

Practice Page

46   Kangaroo

Practice Page

48 Elephant

Practice Page

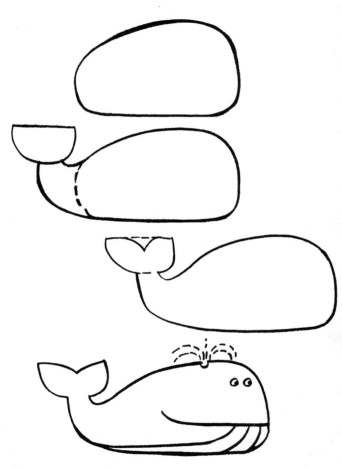

50   Whale

Practice Page

52   Seal

Practice Page

54   Bear

Practice Page

56   Panda

Practice Page

58   Rhinoceros

Practice Page

60 Chimpanzee